Palm Trees and *Raindrops*

Palm Trees And Raindrops
copyright 2020 by Nilson Ramos.
 All rights reserved.

Any inquiries to be sent to info@NilsonRamos.com.
Nilson Ramos
1065 SW 8th St
Unit # 154
Miami, FL 33130

ASIN: B089JQ315P

Library of Congress Control Number: 2020909908
Printed in the United States of America

Book Cover: Karin Romero
         @karinzart

Illustrations: Paul Correa
         @paulcorreart

Editing: S. Marie Vasquez
         @smarie.tv

         Nilson Ramos
         @wordsbynilson

Sharing your thoughts helps us improve our next project.
Any feedback is appreciated. Thank you!

info@NilsonRamos.com

Dedication

I dedicate this book to all of those who have felt lost and no one to turn to.

To those who have had their hearts broken or have broken a heart or two.

To those who have lost hope or caused someone to lose hope.

This is for you.

And know that in the end, everything will be okay.

Forewords

I wouldn't consider myself a romantic or even well versed in the language of love. But I do think that I'm human savvy. What does that mean? It means that I pride myself in understanding human behavior. Body language, tone of voice; all the little things that makes the person tic before they toc.

That being said, this collection of poems dives head first into how love can be the most beautiful thing and/or how it can fuck you all the way up.

The way Nilson tells a story within stories within poems is truly engaging. It shows, in a very relatable way, the joys and perils of love from both points of view. The beautiful way in which you get lost within his words and feel like every situation is personal, shows the time and effort he puts into his craft.

Please enjoy this body of work. Pay attention to all the little things and you'll figure out all the tics before the tocs ....

Adonis Demorizi
@artbysupremo

I'm thankful that these pages exist. For god knows how long I've tried to get Nilson to show his work to the world, which is the only way to grow as an artist. And now, it's finally here. And I hope this is only a first stepping stone, not in a career, but in show-casing his vulnerability through his art.

Now, I'm no poetry fan, so I'm not here as a testament to the art form or the art itself, but to the artist. I've known Nilson for well over 15 years, and as such, I know this man's heart. He can be a heartbreaker, he can be complex, he can also be a dick. But he's a person who refuses to stop believing in his idea of love.

Sure, that might seem foolish sometimes, but I think the world needs more people who dare to be foolish.

Enjoy, and I hope that when you hold this book up, you hold a mirror to your own feelings and understanding.

Elias Serulle
@elijahasa

We have all experienced stories of love gained, love lost, and heartbreak. The journey which we all take transitioning from the days of blissful ignorance in love to the solace which must be taken in again being without. "Palm Trees and Raindrops" is Nilson's literary journey through this. The passion and intensity with which the prose is written, transports you into his shoes and is an apt comparison to what we have all gone through or will go through.

Each morning as we would sit down and have a Cuban coffee prior to really diving into work, Nilson Ramos would allow me a glimpse into the machinations behind what was, unbeknownst to me, becoming " Palm Trees and Raindrops". The visceral truthfulness and passion in our conversations debating the merits of a man and the pitfalls of masculine toxicity. I was honored to be given the opportunity to experience "Palm Trees and Raindrops" prior to its release and connected profoundly with it in the same manner our break time philosophical conversations resonated and connected in me.

Writing is hard by any means, writing with passion is a true art form. What is experienced in "Palm Trees and Raindrops" is above all a journey through Nilson's art. I am certain you will enjoy this journey as much as I did.

-Douglas Matarazzo

Palm Trees and *Raindrops*

Palm Trees and *Raindrops*

This is the story of an iconic couple and their deteriorating love.

And in this romantic tale I share she leaves, and well, never comes back.

God damn did she love him. And he loved her wholly.

It was a mutual love that inspired others, once upon a time.

But like in most romances,

it reached a plateau and it seemed like they didn't know how to

overcome this predestined phase.

They were young and didn't understand love. Does anyone, really?

See, he was her first everything and convinced himself there was only

one solution to their problem, to let her go.

Let her go, let her explore, and being that it is meant to be, he thought,

she will return to her first love.

Better now than later, I suppose.

It broke his heart, but he knew it was necessary.

And in this long, perilous venture,

he was aware that she needed to meet someone else.

And she did.

And he also knew she was going to then miss him

and mourn the confusion she was facing.

And again, error-free.

He was a step ahead of her the entire time, up until the end.

He let her go thinking it was merely the end of a chapter.

If only he knew it was the end of their story.

"I have to go"

were the words she deliberately mumbled.

And that is when I learned- the hard way-

that words aimed directly at the heart

have no time frame for a cure.

I know it has been some time now since your departure,

but see,

it is only now that I have finally accepted that you are gone.

And this is a different, more severe kind of pain from when you left.

It turns out that removing the knife hurts more than the stab itself.

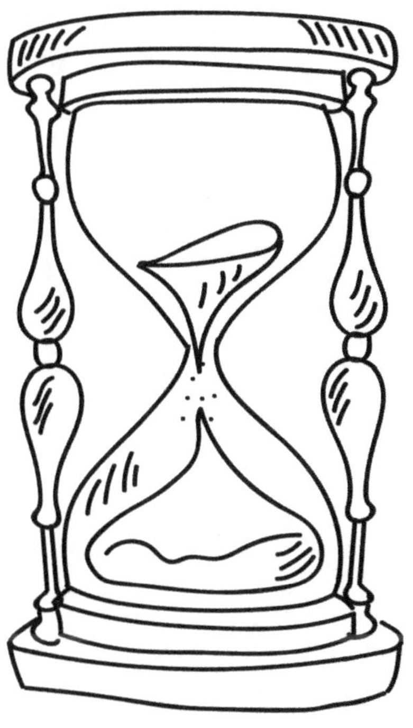

Love ends.

And maybe that is the beauty of it.

How meaningful would love be if there were no ending to it?

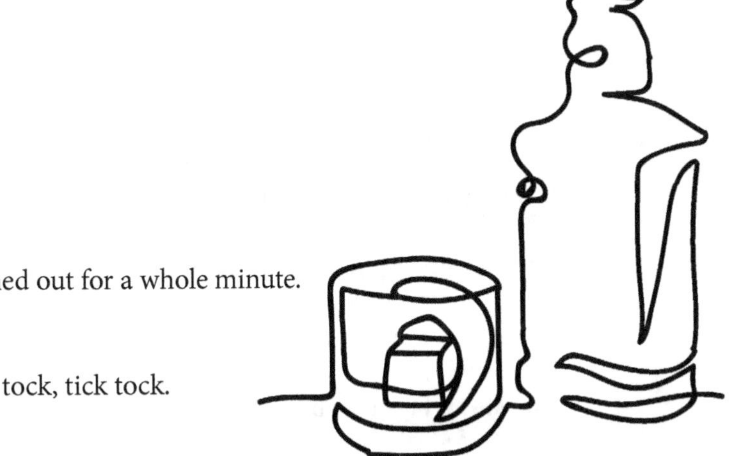

I zoned out for a whole minute.

Tick tock, tick tock.

I snap back to reality.

My fingerprints all over the glass of whiskey on the rocks

I've been slowly gulping down.

I drink to forget,

or maybe I drink to remember...

It wasn't a fairy tale love story

in which the girl meets her prince charming

and the guy is saved by the girl of his dreams.

It was no fictitious bullshit

where they magically live happily ever after together.

But they had something special.

Their eyes spoke to one another in a way so beautifully difficult to understand,

it was highly admirable.

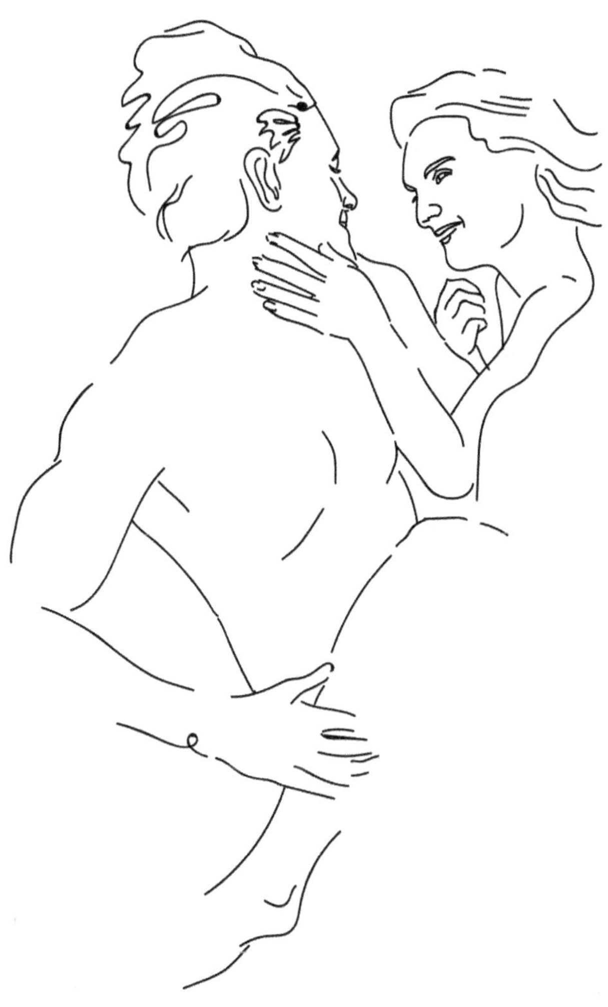

I hear there is no such thing as perfection.

How disrespectful to God...and to us.

I am your water when you are uncontrollably fired up.

You are my water when I am down like a dying plant.

Paradoxically, we can be the same with different purposes.

I am your warmth in the shivering cold.

You are my direction when I seem to be lost.

You see dear, we are each other's final piece to the puzzle.

Perhaps perfect is a strong, exaggerated term

to use to describe our unfathomed love,

but damn are we ideal.

We are fucking exemplary!

If there is any such thing as imperfectly perfect,

or perfectly imperfect,

that is what we are.

Silence was blaring more than ever.

Her sun dress was gloomy

and her movements still like a zombie.

And that's when I knew I lost her.

The echo of her quietness

was louder

than her cry at night.

He knew the end before it began.

He saw her leave before she arrived.

And yet, with the inch of hope he had remaining,

he opened his heart to her,

letting her in where no one else has been before.

Hugged her so tight she vanished from his arms, like a morning mist,

ending exactly how he knew it would.

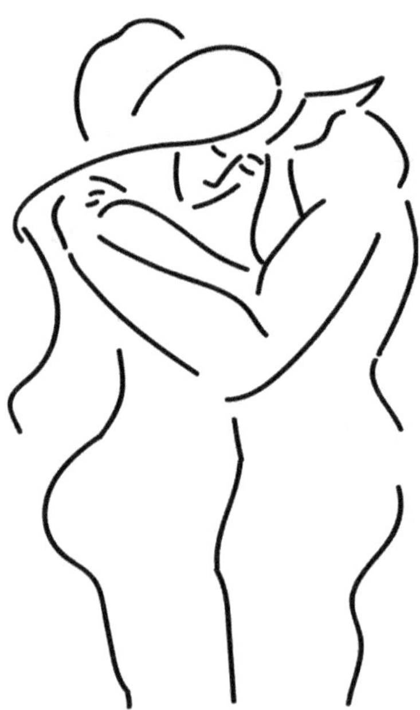

I seemed to always make her laugh,

and that made me happy, to make her happy.

I would gaze at her, at her eyes, her hair, her lips,

admiring her mystique from afar.

I played with her nose and she smiled.

She even added a rare tilt to her smile.

And that's

when it

hit me.

She had met somebody else.

I was knowingly losing her, and I did nothing about it.

We're not blind.

We just choose to see through the truth.

I am in danger of losing myself,

if I haven't already.

I never imagined having to

choose between

two loves,

playing with

two hearts.

Life is tricky.

I fell in love with one,

and grew in love with the other.

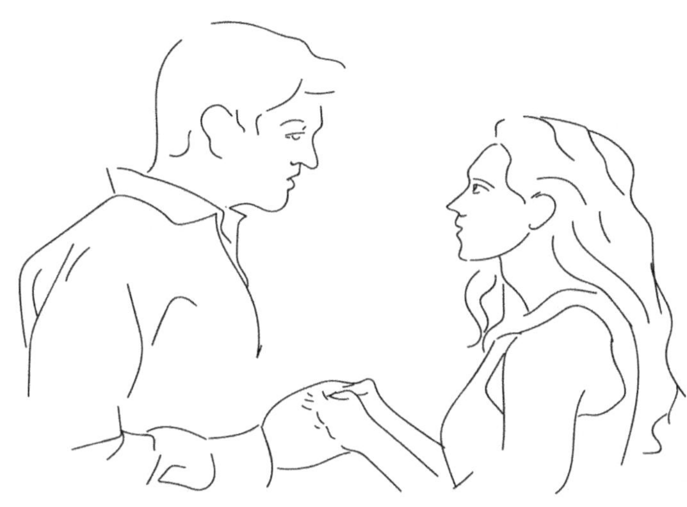

I walked right by her.

She didn't see me,

but I saw her...and him.

And there's no worse feeling

than seeing her

look at him

the same way

she used to look at me.

Hate me if you must.

It would hurt like hell.

It would be dreadful like a long, bad day.

But I know the day will be over and I'll survive.

But showing apathy towards me,

the indifference you convey,

now that can nearly be the death of me.

Palm Trees and *Raindrops*

Those butterflies you once felt in your stomach,

those supposed immutable feelings,

they are gone, blown by the wind.

And I've seen it happen before,

people searching for love in someone else.

And that's the mistake we all make,

we think the wind won't puff those next butterflies away.

We don't know what love is.

It is said that true love is not a feeling, but a decision.

Instead of finding someone, accepting them,

and loving the shit out of them till the end of days,

we want to be in love eternally.

We want to always feel what we felt at the beginning.

And we will never be heartily happy

until we learn the distinction between love and being in love.

Now you find yourself with someone who has everything you have never wanted.

And who knows, maybe he has given you more than I could ever give you.

But I'm okay with knowing that I gave you everything I had.

Here I am loved by a woman

whom I will never love

the way I loved you.

And there you are loving someone

whom will never love you

like I did.

I suppose we both lose

in this cruel beauty we call love.

There is a part of me that wishes her the best

and a part of me that wishes you the worst.

A malicious side that envies you.

I envy you because I was with the lost girl who was trying to find herself.

You are with the woman who knows exactly who she is and what she wants.

I had met her potential, who she could be.

You got the best of her, the best of who she has become.

I remember when she used to live for me, but now she dies for you.

She and I had dreams of a future together,

a future that you and she are now living.

I envy you because I was her first love, and you, you are her last.

I close my eyes and fall deep into a peaceful sleep.

We talk, you tease, I clown.

You laugh at my dumb jokes like a woman in love would.

I smile.

And although I know I would see you later that day,

the hardest part is always saying goodbye.

I kiss your forehead.

You smile.

"I love you", we mutually say, as your hair gently caresses my face.

I wake up and I scratch my face.

Sometimes I still feel your hair lingering around.

Even the most beautiful times come to an end. I wish I knew that back then.

I compel myself back to sleep.

I would rather sleep and dream of you than live a nightmare without you.

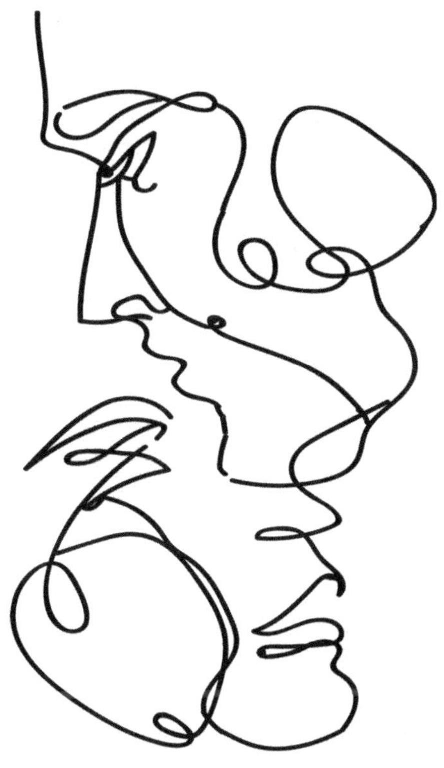

Palm Trees **and** *Raindrops*

I have been missing you.

The thought of how my hands would slip into yours.

How your eyes would smile at me.

I wish I could go back in time

and feel it all over again.

But for now, I'll have to bear with the memories of how I felt.

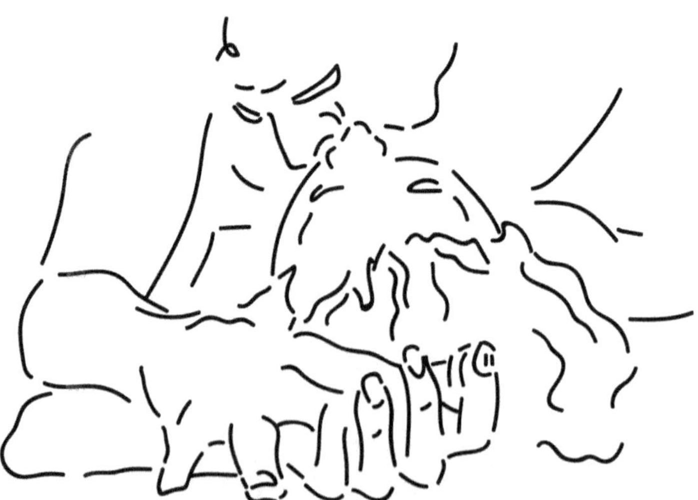

Missing you hurts.

And fuck do I miss you.

Lonely nights sitting abreast my sorrow.

Lonely nights, oh lonely nights,

they hurt.

But damn, that pain doesn't compare to when I'm happy.

My joyous times are my saddest

because my most memorable moments are supposed to be with you.

Instead, you're making your own memories and I'm making mine.

Missing you hurts most in plain sight with the pain hidden behind a fake smile.

She walks in my direction with a brightened face,

radiant as usual.

The same expression she would have when she was in love with me.

She approaches me gracefully.

I can see it in her eyes,

she's been yearning for this moment.

I've been yearning for this moment…

the feeling of a new beginning.

Kiss me.

I have been craving the taste of your warm lips.

Caress me.

I have been longing for the kindness of your gentle touch.

Wipe away my tears,

and avail this moment under the moonlight and make me yours.

Desiring a passion he no longer provides,

imploring for lust that has always connected us,

she pulls me towards her and wraps her legs around my waist.

I'm here to fill a void,

I know that.

I know what I am to you.

But what really matters is what you are to me,

everything.

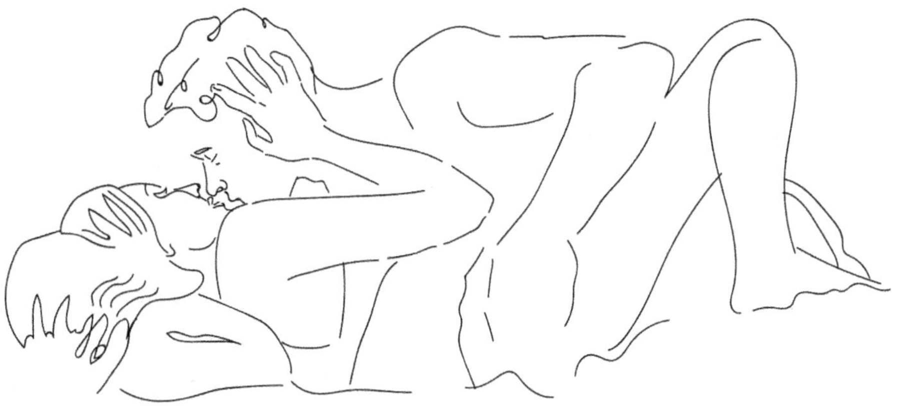

34

Her smile.

That's it, it's her ingenuous smile.

She smiles and that originates everything.

Her smile makes her brown eyes spark,

and when I look into her eyes, smiling back becomes inevitable.

And then she blushes, swings her face away while her smile enlarges.

I pull her closer and hug her.

She clings into my arms, softly rubbing my back with her fingertips.

I hug her tighter and fall in love with her all over again.

And when I tell you I love you

I don't need you to say it back,

especially if you don't feel the same way.

It's just that I learned that

there is no worse way of drowning

than in unspoken words.

It is more than love.

And I ask myself,

Do I hold on

or

do I let go?

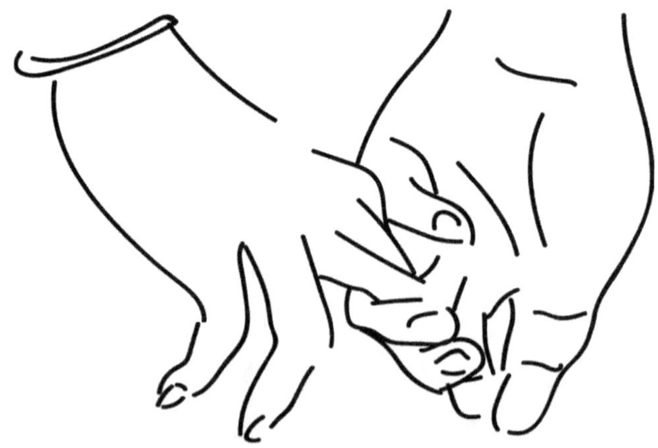

37

Beauty can be heartbreaking.

Heartbreaks can be beautiful.

Saying goodbye isn't always a hug, kiss, or wave.

Sometimes it takes tearing apart the photograph in your wallet

you look at every night,

burning into ashes every love letter ever written,

trashing your favorite gifts,

changing the radio station when the song once dedicated to you comes on,

ignoring your anniversary date when you see it on a clock.

Sometimes goodbyes are letting go of the memories you tightly hold onto

and hoping the memories can someday evanesce and let go of you.

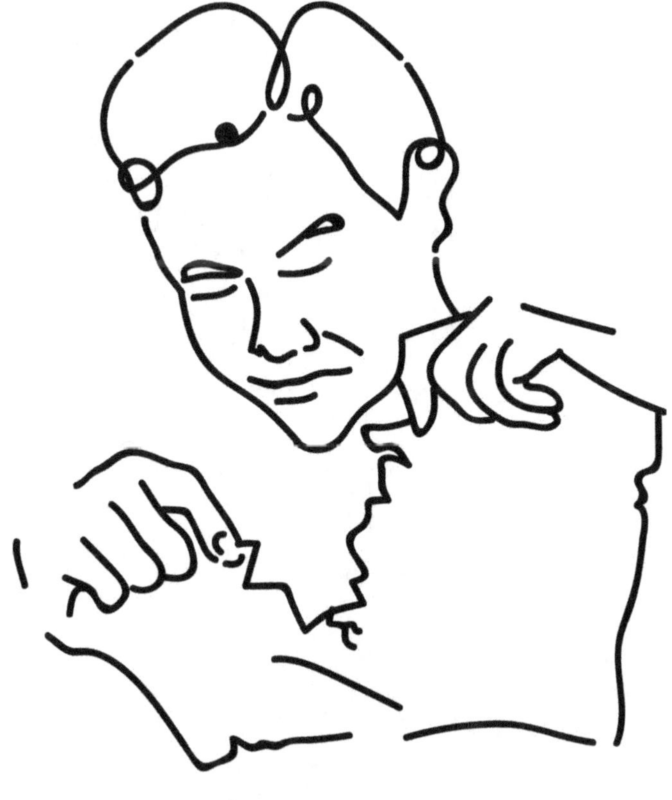

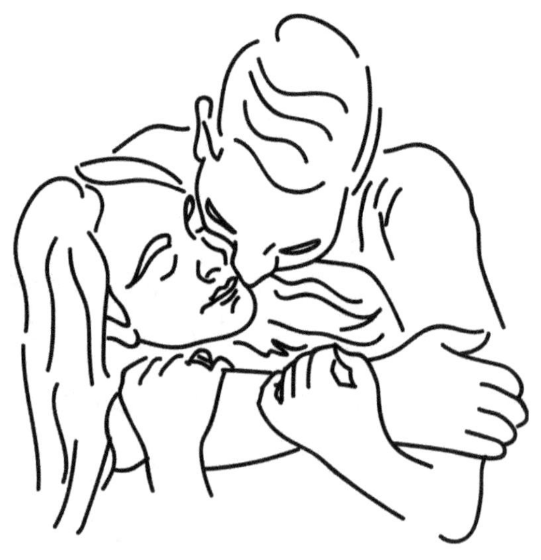

I feel you slipping away

but I can't let go.

I thought our time was up,

but then I think of all the good times we shared…

and the promised good times we have not shared.

I know it is only a matter of time

for you to let go

because I feel you slipping away.

But for now, I just can't let go.

Is it possible we may have loved each other too much?

Maybe we loved each other so much that one mistake,

no matter how big or tiny,

was an unbearable weight to carry,

as we trapped ourselves in an enclosed cage of endless guilt.

"You don't hurt the person you love", we always said, "I will never hurt you".

Maybe we loved each other so much,

we found the strength to forgive one another, but not ourselves.

Maybe we loved each other too much and we didn't love ourselves enough.

I can only wish to see you again.

And as long as we can both look up

and see the same moon,

I will never lose hope.

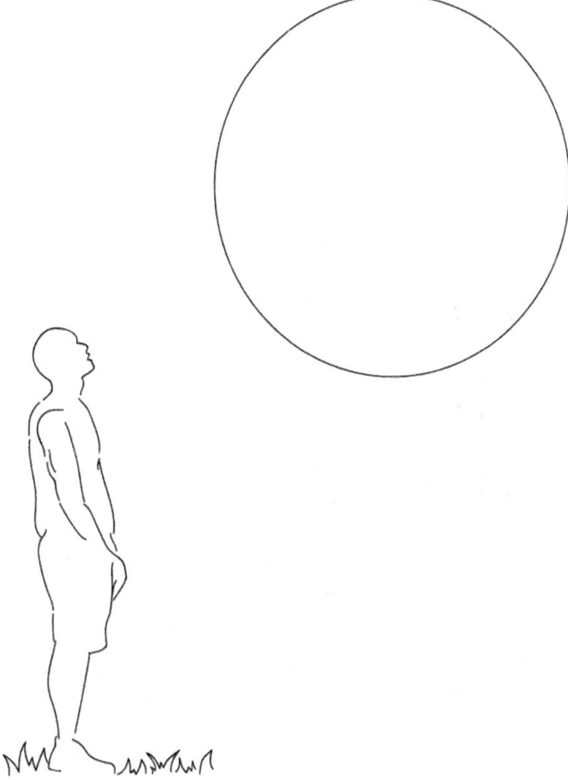

Hope…

The one thing that holds us together.

The one thing that tears us apart.

Fucking hope.

I'm not like those other men,

looking for their lost love,

searching for the one who got away.

I know where to find her,

and perhaps that's what hurts the most.

Every decision I have made

has led me to where I am today.

I've made mistakes.

I've said things I can't take back

and I've done things I can't undo.

And I regret nothing at all

because there was some truth behind

everything said or done at that point in time.

But I am currently in a stage

I never expected to be in.

And I am left with only one question.

When did I blink for a bit too long

to have the moments taken away

and replaced by memories?

Destiny united us

and has now steered us in different directions.

> *I will always wait for you, you say.*

I have always admired that about you,

how hopeful you can be.

There are days I won't ever forget,

nights I will always reminisce about.

Your love was music to my heart.

And as the years go by,

I will continue singing your name.

Lovely past,

uncertain future.

> *I sadly leave knowing you won't always wait for me.*

With an entire audience watching her, all her attention was on me.

She would twirl slowly gazing deeply into my brown, dilated eyes,

as I took a much-needed sip of my ice-cold beer.

It's like she felt my kind heart and pondered over

what a guy like me was doing at a gentlemen's club.

Like if I reflected potential happiness for her.

I stared back, fascinated by her perky breasts and well-formed ass.

Her hips were provocatively sexy, and her face was simply gorgeous.

Money pouring over her body, she found her way closer to me.

I smelled her Victoria's Secret Tease perfume

and felt her heavy breathing on my neck as she danced her hidden pain away.

I placed the beer down and enjoyed my apparent exclusive show.

We were both broken looking to be fixed, just in different ways.

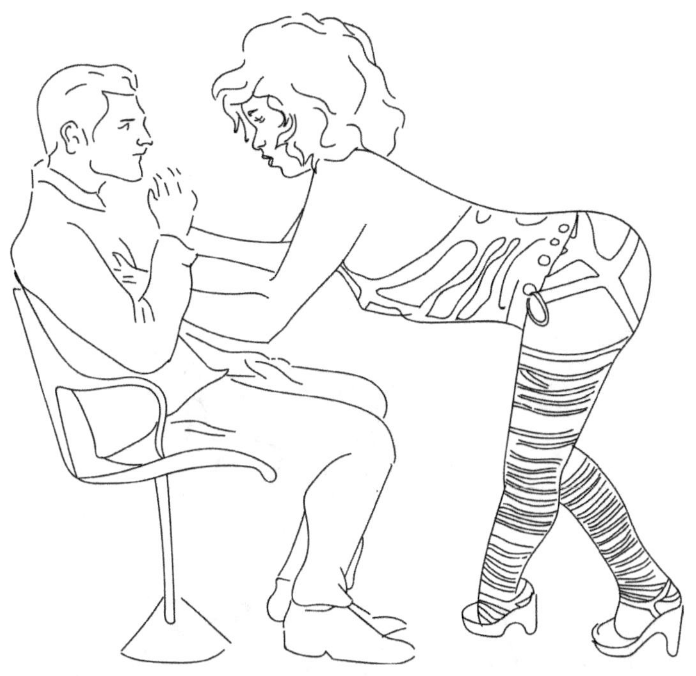

The emptier I am,

the heavier I feel.

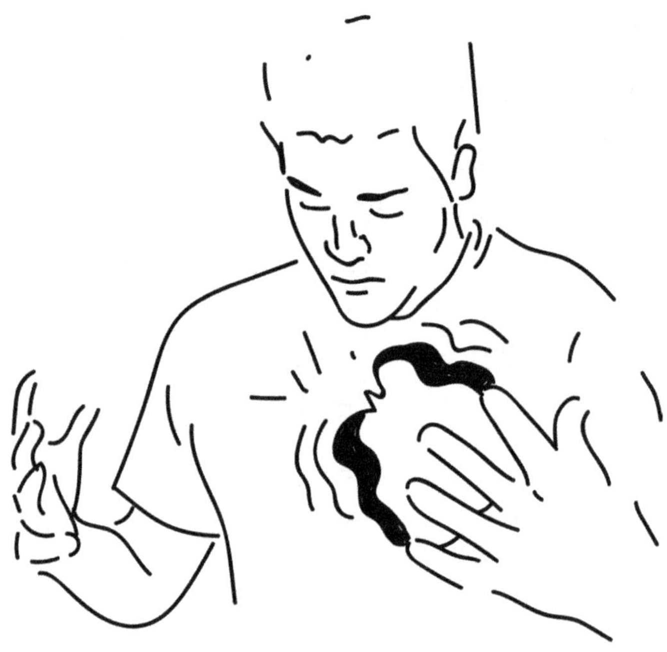

She wiped the white off her nose.

And with sunken eyes, she laughs through the pain.

She's neurotic. Somehow that keeps me around.

She drinks out of the bottle and dances for me.

Diplomático Reserva, her preferred rum.

She parties hard, loves just as intensely.

She's devoted to me,

even if it is only for one night.

Palm Trees and *Raindrops*

Follow your heart, they insisted.

Guided by a bitterly, broken one,

or really, misguided,

I have been fated to go astray.

Hollow soul, hopeless aspirations.

I find myself lost in a world of lust,

sinking in temporary pussy

and half empty bottles.

I invariably thought one can

either bounce back up

from a forceful fall,

or drop flat to a point of affliction

so low there's no recovering.

I never imagined

how tall one can stand

while hitting rock bottom.

53

It wasn't supposed to be like this.

A heart full of warmth and devotion

has turned into shattered pieces of my weakest self.

And now desolation is all I know.

What was once home

is now an unfamiliarity to my heart, to my beliefs.

It wasn't supposed to be like this, yet it is.

Palm Trees and *Raindrops*

It wasn't love, or maybe it was. Maybe we chose to not admit it.

We knew everything about each other, except our past,

which we agreed not to discuss.

Something kept her from commitment,

but her companionship was all I longed-for.

And when she wore pajamas and her long, brown hair was a mess

was when I couldn't keep my eyes off her.

Her beauty was breathtaking.

She felt safe with me; she would say.

Laying her head on my shoulder I would smell another man's cologne,

and I would quietly smirk.

It was okay because at that moment her presence comforted me.

I caught her looking at a blonde hair sitting on my bed.

Oh well, she must have thought.

It wasn't love, or maybe it was. Maybe we chose to not admit it.

Palm Trees and *Raindrops*

I've been warned about women like you.

The ones who desperately need to feel something, anything.

Why must you fix my scruffy eyebrows?

Why bring me coffee to bed wearing that sexy lingerie.

Did I mention that was my favorite?

I've dealt with women like you in the past.

Women who seek company to avoid agonizing loneliness.

Why must you scratch my back knowing that is my absolute weakness?

Why whisper in my ear how great we can be together?

I will not love you, and you know that.

Don't give me your heart.

Don't look at me as if we are destined for one another.

I can fuck you like he never will.

I can have you screaming my name.

But I cannot fix your brokenness.

I refuse to be with you knowing you wish I was him.

I have met your kind before, and I will not fall for you.

Palm Trees and *Raindrops*

As a man who falls in love with scars and the stories behind them,

who debilitates over eyes full of tears and sad conversations following,

I become fond of something dissimilar.

It must be her positive energy and good vibes,

the way she celebrates happiness and smiles at life.

She is unbroken, innocent-minded, oblivious to deceit.

She says she loves me, a subdued fool.

An imbecile who repulses anything too real.

And this, this is not a fantasy, this is real.

I walk away, marking her with disappointment.

She says I broke her heart; I say I saved her soul.

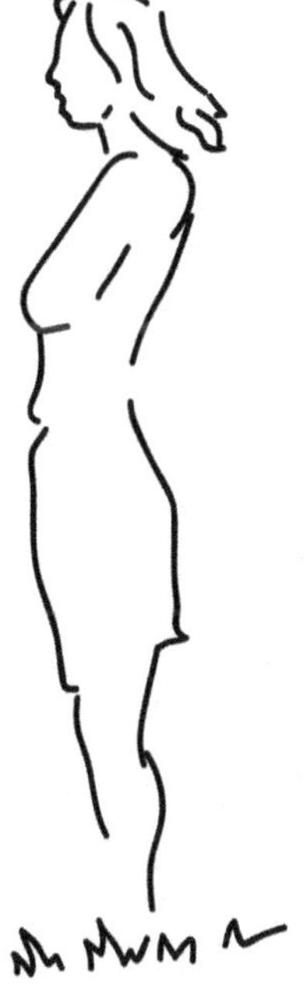 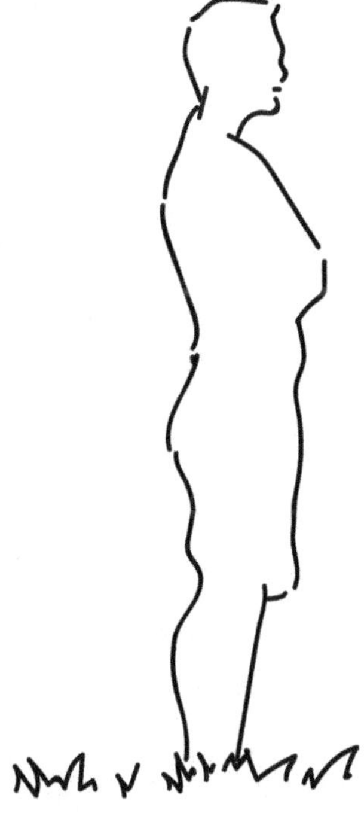

Inconsistency has defined our relationship,

and perhaps I am to blame.

I've come to the realization

that the more passionate the beginning,

the more disastrous the ending.

I am protecting my heart, as well as yours.

59

As a hopeless romantic,

I have always believed the possibility of a happy ending.

But I am starting to realize there is anything but.

Because in your heart, you never quite get over it.

You always carry something with you,

loss, remorse, mistrust…something.

Some people will never be genuinely happy.

And it makes me wonder what is sadder;

the fact that we have what we don't want,

or that we want what we can't have.

Palm Trees and *Raindrops*

I have pushed her away

and it appears almost impossible to lure her back

into what could have been an awe-inspiring love story.

Her skin is as cold as her fortified heart,

and while I intend to gently warm her up, she retreats.

I go on to live with a repentant "what if"

and sigh my way into another chance lost.

I fell in love with her.

We shared a moment and I was enraptured by her sweet smell and soft skin.

But it was just that,

a moment.

I fell in love with who she was and fell out of love with who she wasn't.

She wasn't you.

So many things left unsaid and wrong roads taken.

And I can't help but wonder if these different roads

lead us back to each other and maybe,

just maybe,

our last conversation can prompt the beginning of a love reborn.

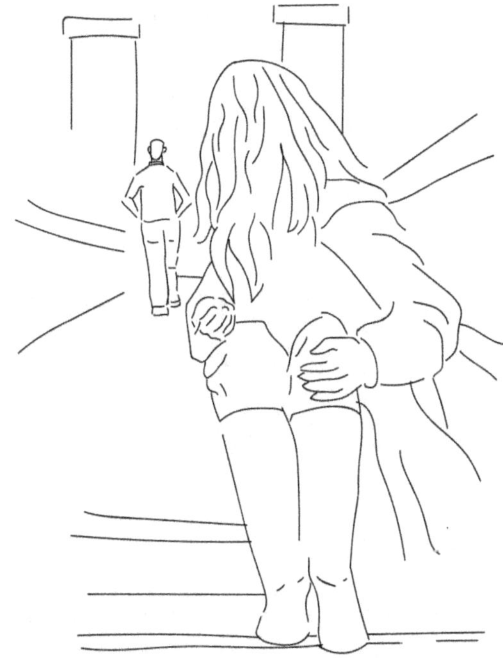

Palm Trees and *Raindrops*

I detest when people say, "I need you".

I find it irritating to hear "I can't live without you".

Those are irrational words, desperate expressions.

But I must admit, life without you is abysmal.

It fucking sucks.

With you, the sunset is a resplendent view

that beholds our deep conversations and uncontrollable smiles

as we stare profoundly into each other's eyes.

Without you, the sunset is a mere reminder of just another day gone.

With you, falling is momentum to get back up.

Without you, falling is plain failure.

With you, I laugh under the rain until we bump into a movie-type kiss.

Without you, the sound of the raindrops is as depressing as the memories

that come to mind of our sinking love.

With you, a drink is a celebration.

Without you, a drink is a remedy for a bitter moment.

I don't need you, but I am the best version of myself with you.

I can live without you, but I would prefer not to.

Although the odds may be against us,

and we run into obstacles blocking our way,

and time solely tells us we are preordained

to walk different paths,

you are always here with me,

in my mind anyway,

and in my heart,

where you belong.

I want you to know that I understand everything you have risked

and every tough choice you have had to make.

I selflessly put myself in your shoes and realize

we are all humans fighting different battles.

And when it seems overly complicated or illogical to understand you,

I accept you.

Because if love were to be defined in one word,

love is acceptance.

Palm Trees and *Raindrops*

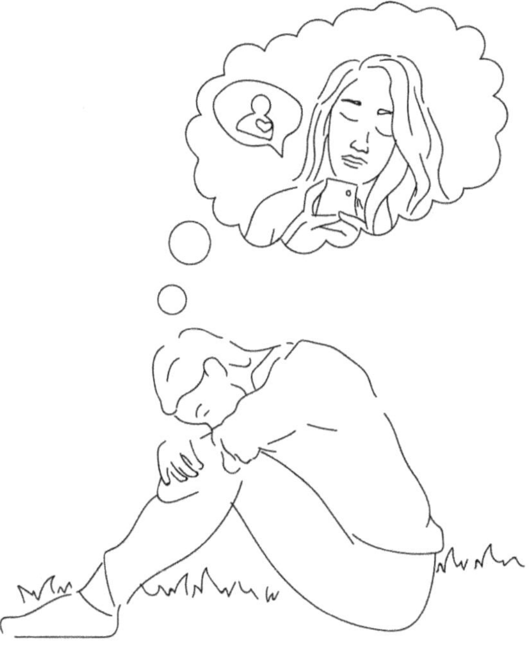

I taste your soul on my lips

as I whisper your name underneath my breath.

You wander endlessly in my mind,

reigning in my emotions.

I don't know if we have reached our end

and I'll have to conform to just the thought of you,

but all I can do is wonder,

do *you* think of me?

You don't forget your first love.

I never will, anyway.

But I took a wrong turn somewhere,

and I'm left questioning myself.

Will my first love forget me?

What you are used to is potent.

What you are used to is so potent

it can easily be confused with love;

you get accustomed to someone's company and convince yourself you love them.

What you are used to is potent.

What you are used to is so potent

it can even overpower love;

no matter how much you love someone, it is possible to adapt to their absence.

And any story that ends with someone being with the wrong person or alone

because of what you are used to,

is a sad fucking story.

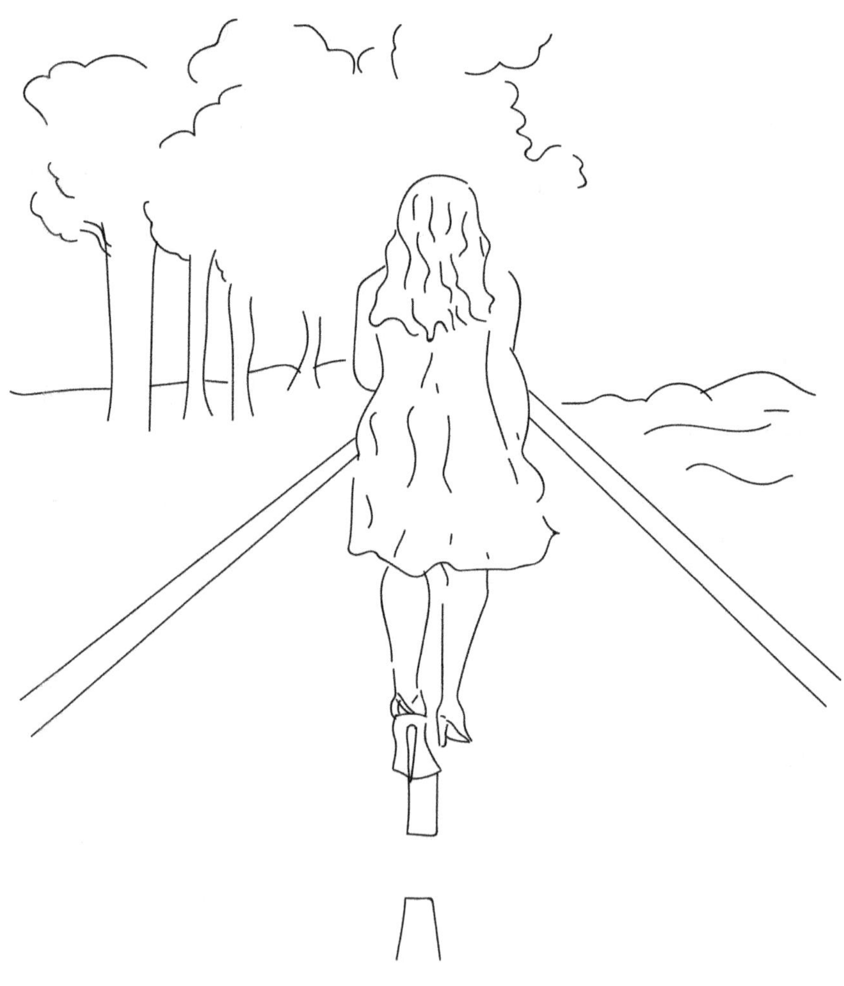

And if it is true what they say

that

all roads lead home,

then

home is what you are.

ABOUT THE AUTHOR

Nilson Ramos, based in Miami, Florida is a poet and storyteller who grew up between the Dominican Republic and the New York/ New Jersey area. He travels extensively, where he finds most of his inspiration. His passion for writing has led him to write songs and different types of poetry, mostly free verse.

NilsonRamos.com

@wordsbyNilson

www.ingramcontent.com/pod-product-compliance
Lightning Source LLC
Chambersburg PA
CBHW070554160726
48003CB00005B/2049